WATERMARK

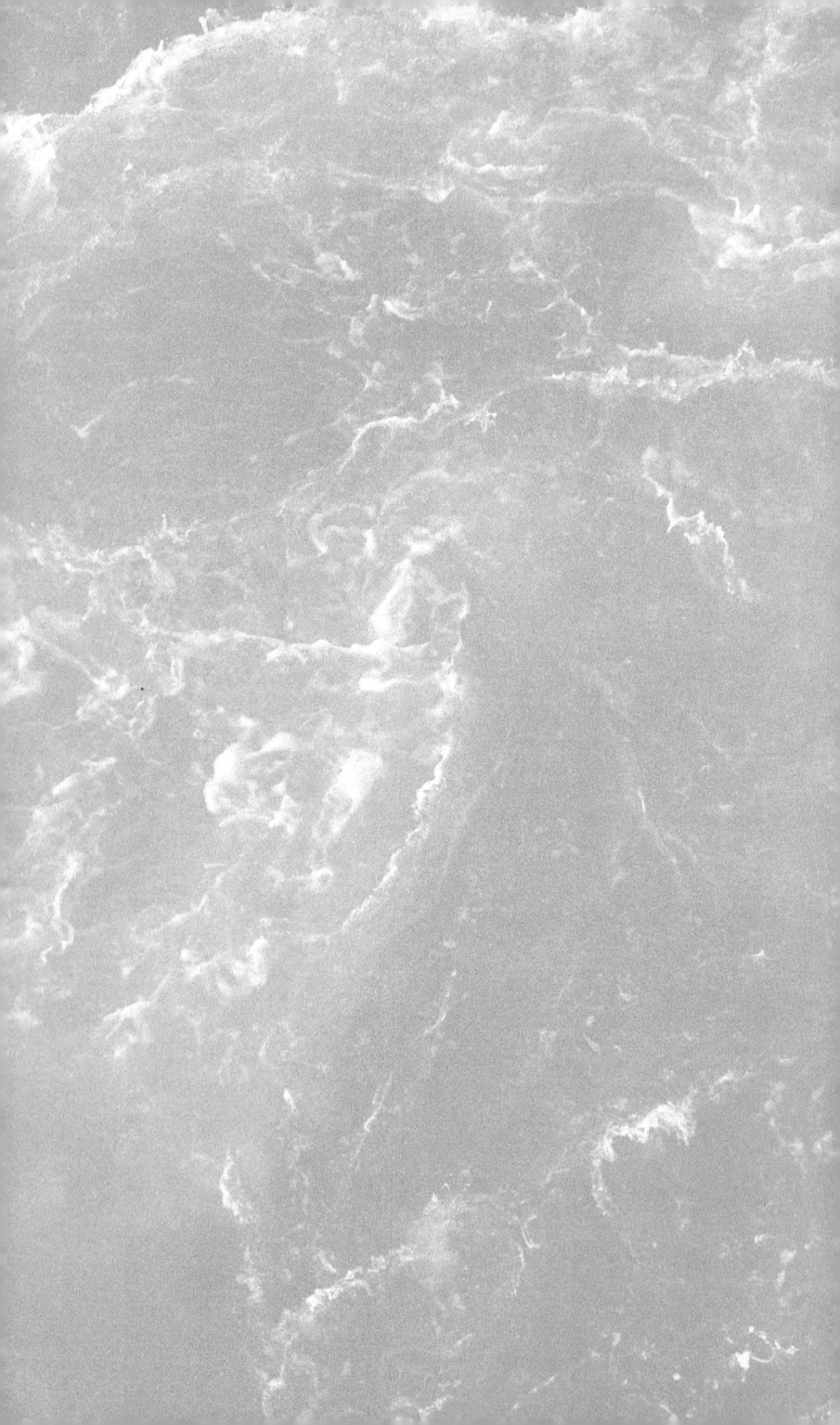

ADVANCE PRAISE

"Like a hand reaching to pull the drowning from deep water, Barbara Sabol's book of portraits reclaims the lost voices of the Great Johnstown Flood: working class lives she precisely renders with a polyvocal and beautiful tenderness."
—Sean Thomas Dougherty, author of *The Dead Are Everywhere Telling Us Things*

"'Dressmaker, scullery maid, drifter, carpenter, millwright, mother, / the children whose dreams scatter in the grass, *you are not forgotten*' in Barbara Sabol's *Watermark*. These vivid poems rise from the floodwaters of 1889 Johnstown, Pennsylvania, carrying with them the variously imagined voices and stories of a fully realized town. This is poetry of witness at its finest—present and fierce."
—Marcela Sulak, author of *City of Skypapers* and *Mouth Full of Seeds*

"In its beautifully woven poems, *Watermark* gives voice to those lost voices of the 1889 Johnstown Flood, telling the stories of loss, devastation, and the slow process of healing and recovery. Barbara Sabol has painted a masterful, moving portrait of time and place in the regional spirit and tradition of Edgar Lee Masters' *Spoon River Anthology* and E. A. Robinson's *Tilbury Town* poems. *Watermark* is a significant addition to the canon of Northern Appalachian poetry."
—William Scott Hanna, poetry editor, *Northern Appalachia Review*

"Using a variety of forms—among them ballad, golden shovel, triolet, erasure, and epistle—Barbara Sabol crafts a lyric remembrance of one of America's greatest disasters. Sabol not only evokes the voices of the perished and survivors, but also of memorable figures of the times. More often, readers hear from common people. In 'The Carpenter,' the title character is described as a tattooed 'fighter' who discovers on the last day of May over 130 years ago, 'For all my mass, I was no match for that water's brawn, its gnarled fist.' *Watermark* rises to give voice to an event now gone from living memory. It is a substantial poetic achievement that rewards readers on every page."
—Jerry Wemple, author of *We Always Wondered What Became of You*

WATERMARK

Poems of the Great Johnstown Flood of 1889

Barbara Sabol

Alternating Current Press
Boulder, Colorado

Copyright © 2023 Barbara Sabol
All rights reserved

Published by Alternating Current Press
Boulder, Colorado 80302
altcurrentpress.com
All rights reserved

Library of Congress Control Number: 2023947752
ISBN-13 (paperback): 978-1-946580-41-2
ISBN-10 (paperback): 1-946580-41-4
ISBN-13 (hardcover): 978-1-946580-42-9
ISBN-13 (ebook): 978-1-946580-43-6

Interior and cover design: Leah Angstman
Author photo: Melanie Rae Buonavolonta © 2023

The following is a work of fiction created by the author. All names, individuals, places, items, brands, events, characters, &c., are the product of the author's imagination, are used fictitiously, or are entirely coincidental.

No part of this publication may be reproduced, stored in a retrieval system, or transmitted, in any form or by any means, electronic, mechanical, photocopied, recorded, or otherwise, without the prior permission of Alternating Current Press, except for the quotation of brief passages used inside of an article, criticism, or review.

Printed in the United States of America

10 9 8 7 6 5 4 3 2 1

TABLE OF CONTENTS

At the Plot of the Unknowns 23

I. _____ RAIN _____ 25

At the South Fork Fishing and Hunting Club 27
The Stargazer 29
Fishing the Stonycreek 30
Keeping an Eye on the River 31
As the Storm Bears Down 32
By Noon, That Last Day of May 1889 34
Getting the Message Through 35
John Hess Ties the Engine Whistle Down 37
The Day Express 39
On Hearing John Hess' Engine Whistle 40
The Drifter 41
In This Final Spinning Minute 42

Waterwheel 47

II. _____ WAVE _____ 49

Hettie Ogle, Western Union Telegraph Operator . . . 51
The Scullery Maid 53
The Bookseller 54
A Pool of Tears 55
The Lost Children 57
Miss Elizabeth Bryan 58
The Carpenter 60
Sacramental 61
The Dressmaker 62
To turn a pair of kid shoes 64
Little Shaver 65
The Season of Water 67
The Blue Door 70

Next to me 73

III. _____ **CARRY** _____ 75

After two days I return 77
Dear Father, ... 79
Colonel Unger, Returning to the Clubhouse 82
Clara Barton at Her Dressing Table 84
Flood and Fire 86
Once the Floodwaters Recede 87
The Saints Have Faces of Stone 88
Tired   I walk toward everything 89
Ballad of the Makeshift Morgue 90
The Errant Husband 91
Attempting to Speak of Home 93
The Poison of Her Mourning 95

⁓

Summer along the Stonycreek 99

IV. _____ **FLOW** _____ 101

After Ruin 103
My Dearest Madeleine, ... 105
Clara Barton Reports from the Field 107
Out of Ruin 109
John Hess' Last Day 110
Interview on the Ten-Year Anniversary
 of the Johnstown Flood 111
Against Consolation 113
I Washed into the World 114

⁓

Matter:

Advance Praise 3
Map of Johnstown 12
Foreword 17
End Notes 117
About the Author 119
Acknowledgments 121
Author Thanks 123
Colophon 125

dedicated to every last lost voice

Here lies one whose name was writ in water
—Epitaph on Keats' tombstone, February 24, 1821

> *But, oh, to live awhile as marrow*
> *in someone else's bones,*
> *to breathe her breath upon the mirror*
> *held up to your life*
> —Pauletta Hansel, "So Maybe It's True"

Do memories of the living build
Memory-houses of the dead,
A place at heart where we may meet?
—Kathleen Raine, "On a Deserted Shore"

NINEVEH

Y K

CONEMAUGH
FURNACE

CONEMAUGH RIVER

SANG HOL

BIRD'S-EYE VIEW
OF THE
CONEMAUGH VALLEY,
FROM NINEVEH TO THE LAKE.

JOHNSTOWN, PA.

From personal Sketches and Surveys of the Pennsylvania R. R., by permission.

ALEX. Y. LEE,
ARCHITECT AND CIVIL ENGINEER, PITTSBURGH, PA.

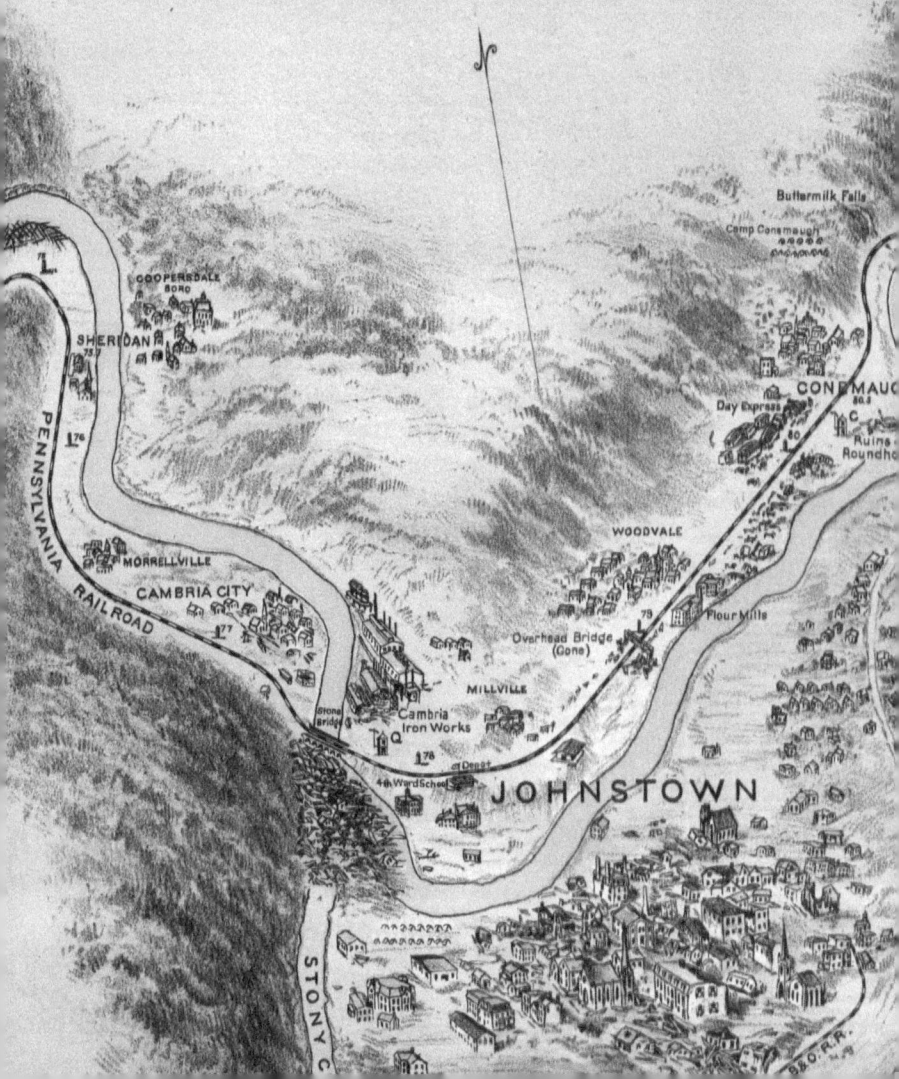

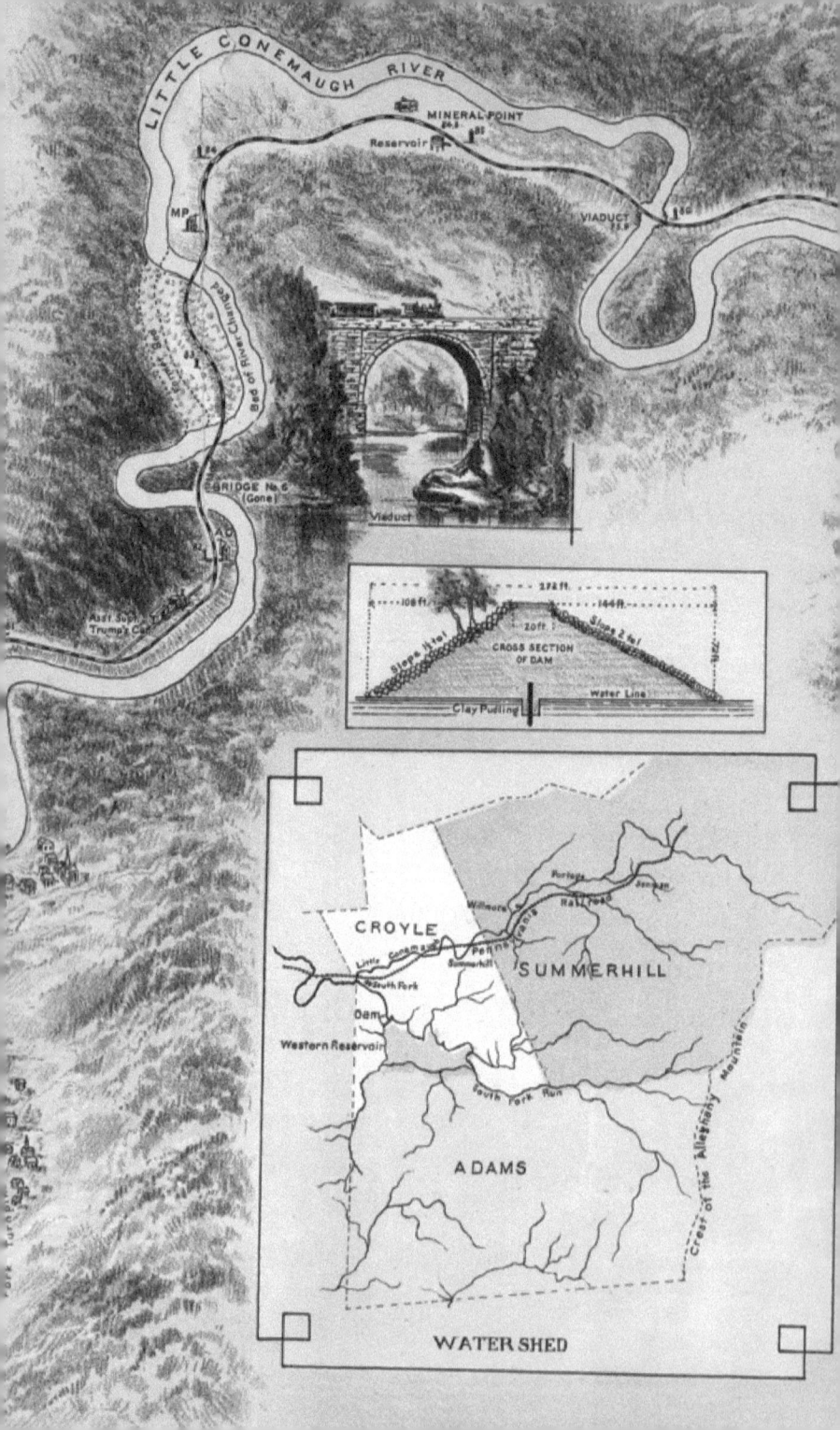

SOUTH FORK DAM

FOREWORD

Johnstown is my hometown, and I had been familiar with the flood story all my life. Then, one morning in May of 2019, as I read the original morgue book in gloved hands, taking in the often disturbingly explicit descriptions of the flood victims, I knew that I would write this book.

Known for its mineral wealth and the quality of its steel, Johnstown, Pennsylvania, had transformed into a thriving industrial city by the late nineteenth century. The Cambria Iron Works, a model for modern iron and steel production, was one of the nation's largest producers of steel rail. As the mill grew in size and reputation, an immigrant population seeking work grew in like proportion.

Johnstown is situated in a river valley in the foothills of the Alleghenies. Fourteen miles upstream of the city, an abandoned reservoir was transformed into Lake Conemaugh, a mountain resort lake, enjoyed by members of the exclusive South Fork Fishing and Hunting Club. Its membership included the steel, railroad, and banking magnates of the day—those who profited from the industry in the valley city below.

On the afternoon of May 30, 1889, after a splendid Decoration Day parade, the heaviest rainfall ever recorded east of the Rockies began, triggering what came to be known as "The Great Flood." While swollen rivers and creeks narrowed by industrial waste and snowmelt from the mountains contributed to the flooding, the chief cause was the poorly maintained resort lake. Damaged discharge pipes were sold for scrap and never replaced; the spillway clogged with debris due to installation of a weir to enhance sport fishing; and the lake was heightened by three feet, but the spillway was never widened to accommodate the increased volume of water.

In a matter of 45 minutes, industry, homes, and a town's population were swept into the history book of great disasters. The dam holding back 20,000,000 tons of water collapsed. A wall of water and debris reached an estimated height of 40 feet and traveled at the velocity of Niagara Falls as it powered through hillside towns and into the city of Johnstown.

More than 2,000 people perished, a third of them never identified. The largest civilian loss of life in the country at that time. Their fate is recorded in the official morgue book, a ledger listing the dead by morgue and number, with a description of physical features, clothing, and condition of the body. Each portrayal was also printed on a coffin-lid tag so that survivors could identify the bodies of their loved ones.

The entries in the morgue book, especially those of the unidentified victims, compelled me to create this chorus of voices. Page upon page of elegant cursive: each detailed morgue account represents a life cut short in an inconceivably tragic fashion. Each an inspiration to give voice, albeit an imagined one, to those "coffined" without a name. Each a call to reanimate the cast of figures in the event—those lost, the survivors, and those instrumental to the historical narrative. This lyric reimagining of the Johnstown Flood of 1889 has renewed and deepened my connection to my hometown, my regard for its remarkable history and the resilience of its people.

Barbara Sabol

WATERMARK

At the Plot of the Unknowns

> *—One of every three bodies found after the Johnstown Flood of 1889 was never identified.*

I belong to a family of grave tenders—we arrive with grass shears, watering cans, season upon season.

A seashell placed on a neighboring stone, small plastic farm animal on the next, say *you are not forgotten*.

After tamping the annuals, I kneel back, conjure my mother. If there is an after, I hope she is pleased with these small gestures.

The day is radiant. Mica and quartz glisten monuments along the path to the plot of the unknown drowned

whose identical marble stones rise from the ground in narrow rows like sheaves of some strange crop.

Their blank faces marked only by weather. Names *writ in water*.

Dressmaker, scullery maid, drifter, carpenter, millwright, mother, the children whose dreams scatter in the grass, *you are not forgotten*.

I lean my full weight on one stone, knowing in my own bones there is a story here, and under the next and the next.

The earth begins to warm. An elusive wood thrush flutes. Crocuses open to the light.

I.
RAIN

I possess neither mind nor heart,
but run with memory beyond the Ark,
its great animal commotion. I am created
to spill.

At the South Fork Fishing and Hunting Club

—July 4, 1888

Morgue Entry: *From Clubhouse. Female. ...*
Fair complexion. Long black hair. Blue dress.
Plain hoop ring, one set on left hand. Blood set.

After a holiday feast of potted game and succulent black bass
a dark-haired woman wanders out to the porch draped with bunting
to watch boaters glide across Lake Conemaugh, a warm wind
guiding skiffs clear to the dam's lip, where she has many times sailed
and looked down upon factory life in Johnstown.

Smokestack plumes would dissolve before reaching
her mountain haven. The idea of this peaceful lake spilling
down the hillside, leaving no more than a muddy crater in the earth,
and in less than a year's time, is beyond her imagining.

She drifts back inside as the sun's buttery glow
drips the last of itself through the open casement window
glossing the fruit strewn on the side table. The day's warmth
held inside the dark grapes' thin skin.

Guests are gathering for dessert—women in light
twill skirts, trimmed with satin piping, men in tailored suits
of worsted cloth, linen collars and cuffs. Among them her intended,
handsome in his blue silk necktie. Next spring, she will visit
the dressmaker in town all the women are raving about.

Mr. McKee, her father's banking associate, invites her to slice
Cook's Independence cake, made with 20 pounds of flour,
10 pounds of butter, a quart of wine and one of brandy.
She claims a slice where the frosting is dressed with rose leaf.

Moving away from the ladies' circles of pleasantries—
the magic of fireworks over the water; the latest tonics—
she admires how the peaches in their silver bowl glow
like small downy sunsets in the low light; how Rome beauties
blush deeper arranged on the white linen cloth, like a still life.

Her father cuts into the enormous green melon shipped
all the way up from Florida in a refrigerated railcar.
It had looked more creature than fruit, primordial almost,
but she believes it must have arrived from the table of the gods
after that first sweet bite.

The Stargazer

> Morgue Entry: *Male. Age 14. Light complexion. Regular features. ... Short, grey knee breeches. Large aquiline nose. Blue eyes. Fine, intelligent, and pleasing look. No shoes or stockings.*

The studs of Orion's belt bright enough this clear,
cold night to trace, connecting the stars from buckle
to sword. The nebulae, midway down—a misty globe
of young stars—right at the tip of my finger.

At tonight's library lecture, the image
of a sixty-minute exposure (imagine!)
showed stars too faint to be seen from earth.
Light years away, the lecturer said. *Light years.*

In that moment my chair lost its hold
on the floorboards. Everything in the hall
blurred, and I felt lifted up and out of my own skin.
Spun like a human nebula.

I can't even describe the feeling. But walking home,
I was still a little wobbly, like that time I stole
a couple swigs from Pop's bottle.

Pop tells me to get my head out of the clouds.
Set my sights on the steel industry, building
railroads, cities. The possibilities, he keeps saying,
are endless.

What ignites me could not be farther
from what he goes on about. His life's given over
to what's dug from the earth—iron ore and coal
lodged beneath these mountains.

But far up, above the chimneys and smokestack fumes
whirling like chalk dust, are whole entire worlds
we don't even know. Endless worlds.

Fishing the Stonycreek

—Decoration Day, May 30, 1889

*After the painting "Fishing on the Conemaugh"
by George Hetzel*

Hip-high in this cold mountain creek, alone
with my own good company. That's all I require.
Nothing but the current ripple, chickadees calling
back and forth from the hemlocks. My casting rod
and a pocketful of spinners and craw jigs.

Here, I'm delivered from the never-ending drone
of the saw blade cutting through the pine. White pine,
tall and straight as any man could hope
to carry himself.

Sun's high, glittering the water and baking the nip
out of my bones. Nothing but damn chill rain here lately.
Let everyone and his uncle crowd into town
for the parade and cheer for their reed bands
and wagons full of old Union soldiers.

Give me solitude and smallmouth bass swirling
in the bug bait. Water's high as ever I've seen it.
After all these days of rain the current's swift, whipped up
with eddies. My read is to cast out long to the cobbled bank,
then walk it down the shoal.

I could plant myself in this creek for hours, breathing in
that sweet mineral water and pine sap, the sun warm
on my neck. Easy enough to hold still and wait. In time,
the bass will leap. There! A gold dorsal fin rising
to the surface. A quick snap on the line and now
it's just that fish and me and this mountain stream.

Keeping an Eye on the River

Emma Ehrenfeld, telegrapher, South Fork Depot, May 31, 1889

The river's already swollen at 7 a.m.
when I climb the depot tower stairs, drenched
as a river rat.

The same showers that soothed me to sleep
turned fierce, a downpour the railroad men
said they'd never seen the likes of.

Engine 1165 idles on the south siding;
no going on with washouts on the tracks
east and west of South Fork.

Conductor and his engineer pace in and out of my office,
awaiting dispatch orders, watching the weather,
the rising river. Nearly out of its banks by noon.

I tend to my sounder, anxious for a clear circuit,
the familiar clicks, and keep the brewer on the flame—
strong black coffee, by the potful.

Not one of us mentions the dam, its flaws, the likelihood
of a breach. Discourse enough, the drumming rain,
the back-and-forth thumping of gum boots.

As the Storm Bears Down

> *John Parke, South Fork Fishing and Hunting Club engineer, the morning of the flood, May 31, 1889*

> *This is the Hour of Lead—*
> *Remembered, if outlived,*
> *As Freezing persons, recollect the Snow—*
> *First—Chill—then Stupor—then the letting go—*
> —Emily Dickinson, "Poem 372"

I awakened to a day draped in gauze—
late-spring snow heaped upon
one-hundred days of rain and still
more rain pummels the lake, swirling
with brush, logs, sawmill planks.
From the clubhouse porch I judge
the water's gained another two feet.
Sluice disabled; the lake's bound to crest.
Here at last, my long-held dread—
this is the hour of lead—

the specter of flood. Past prayer, still
I implore, and row to the lake's far edge.
Stunned to witness stormwater racing
from hills to creeks to lake, mounting
by the minute. I fight the current back
to shore. The pressure must be relieved!
I exhort every able man to dig, clear
layers of debris, divert the water's course.
Our day of reckoning's arrived—
remembered, if outlived.

Picks strike through riprap, shovels scrape,
fling bits of dirt, while horse and plow
strain. Even Club President Unger has
rolled his sleeves to trench a spillway.
All efforts are in vain. The current gains
speed, while the hard-packed earth holds.
Our shouts drowned by the storm—just
rushing water and ring of metal against rock.
I will forever hear it, that discordant echo
as freezing persons recollect the snow.

Now the lake slips over the lip of the dam,
down the hill, into the path of town. A thin flow
at first, gathering force. The dam will soon give!
I gallop the washed-out road, and reach the men
at Heiser's store, who've heard such warnings
before. They shrug off the news even though
their homes, their *lives* are at risk, but swear
they'll get word to the telegraph depot. I ride
to higher ground, lamenting the fate of those below—
first—chill—then stupor—then the letting go—

By Noon,
That Last Day of May 1889

By noon, the tongue is herbed in the soak—
a proper meal for the mister this evening.
After Tom's third double shift at work,
a feast sweetened with basil Ann had been saving.

Next door, a proper meal of mutton this evening.
Seven children to squeeze 'round the table.
Midday, the missus hangs the joint she was saving
for a daughter's birthday; for her doll, a new cradle.

No more children around the Fitzgibbons' table.
The mister and missus plan a quiet supper
to celebrate their anniversary: thirty years in all.
By noon, the jelly is strained with loaf sugar.

The baker's wife plans light fare for their dinner—
cleaned out of pastries at the holiday parade.
By noon, she's rolled out four dozen biscuits;
with a ladle of gravy, the meal's good as made.

Still humming "The Battle Hymn" from yesterday's parade,
by noon, the miner's wife pulps vegetable marrow.
Her hand trembles on the ladle, ever more afraid
of the long rain drumming against her window.

By noon, Ann simmers her stock of bone marrow.
She frets about Tom in this storm after work,
as rain and wind now rattle the windows.
The stewpot seasoned, herbed tongue in the soak.

Getting the Message Through

Emma Ehrenfeld, telegrapher, South Fork Tower

12:00 p.m.

A man comes stomping up into the depot tower,
a shiftless local character, all reared up about a message
he says was given to him by a young fellow who rode
on horseback, down from Lake Conemaugh, hollering:
Water rising, the dam ready to burst!

Well, it sounds a mite suspect—nothing down on paper.
The report might have arisen from drink and hearsay,
but the only way to err at this moment is on the side
of prudence.

Tapping my key at double speed to no avail—wires
must be pulled down by the rush of high water. But one
circuit's open—to operator Pickerell at Mineral Point.

He says his lines west are also down, so the two of us
fix up a message:

*WATER LEVELS CRITICAL. NOTIFY THE PEOPLE
OF JOHNSTOWN.*

He'll write up the note, hand it off to a trackman
to run it, fast as feet can fly, down the track.

1:52 p.m.

*THE WATER IS RUNNING OVER THE BREAST OF THE LAKE DAM,
IN CENTER AND WEST SIDE AND IS BECOMING DANGEROUS*

is the second message from my tower. We've had news
that water has reached the height of the dam, has started to spill.
Sending the report on to Pickerell. Lord knows if there'll be
a runner there to deliver it.

From the tower window, I see the South Fork Creek's risen
up to the first floor of some houses. We could be washed away
from this storm alone. So wild now, pines and aspens
on the hillside banks bend to its power.

2:25 p.m., South Fork

THE DAM IS BECOMING DANGEROUS AND MAY POSSIBLY GO

reads my third and most urgent message to Mineral Point. A rider
from the lake saw water streaming from the center of the dam.
Pickerell has managed to raise a wire, so word can be telegraphed
direct to the yardmaster at East Conemaugh. From there, on to Johnstown.

I keep watch. The creek's churning as if on the boil. I feel more helpless
than ever I expect to again. If I should survive. God forgive me.
Prayer seems useless at this hour. I stay fixed at the edge of my chair.
Remind myself to breathe. Nothing in my lap but my clenched hands.
I wait for the next rush of news through my door.

John Hess Ties the Engine Whistle Down

> *I wanted to whistle something peculiar so that people would take some heed to it.*
> —John Hess, engineer, Pennsylvania Railroad

The Stonycreek's rising—higher and more stirred up
like none of us railroaders ever seen before.
Washouts up and down the tracks; landslides
to clear in every compass direction.

I've been shuffling orders, like a bad poker hand. No rest
for my work train this forenoon. Been hauling a crew
with shovels and picks to clean out slides, fast as the storm
can push mud back between the rails.

Not two hundred yards from the AO tower a flagman waves us
to a halt, saying the north track's in the river.
So, we head up to the big cut, 'til the track runs out—
a wash clear up above the ties.

I leave my engine while the crew clears the tracks,
race on foot to the AO tower, detail the conditions,
then hightail it back to my engine, soaked through. My heart
beatin' like a rabbit with a hound at its heels.

Then I ease the train down to Buttermilk Falls, and after a short time,
I hear it, what we've been dreading but didn't ever believe possible—
a roar like a hurricane through wooded country. No mistaking.
The flood's upon us.

I open the throttle around the bend, southward
toward Johnstown and pull my whistle wide open.
It shrieks continuous—a wail folks around here know
is a warning from engine 1124.

Not but five hundred yards ahead of that wave. Nothing left
but to steam her back up the line, whistle blowing all the way.
Then, by God, I see the tracks below East Conemaugh
washed into the river.

Best I know to do now is pull to a stop, tie that cord down,
and jump from my cab. I round up my crew, hollering,
"Just leave them tools!" and we break for higher ground.
That whistle screaming like there's no tomorrow.

The Day Express

The Day Express, packed with travelers,
steams east along the swollen river
when a washout from incessant rain
and word of flooding stall the train—
held on the tracks five endless hours.

Confusion grips the passengers
as whispers of a dam break scatter.
All wires downed; no news obtained.
On the Day Express, the frantic travelers

soon persuaded by the porters
to clear, and quick, the coach parlor
as the shriek of Hess' engine
signals a wave down the mountain.
Not a moment then to waver or pray
for the Day Express, its fated travelers.

On Hearing
John Hess' Engine Whistle

—Emma Ehrenfeld, telegrapher, South Fork Tower, 3:08 p.m., May 31, 1889

Any operator worth her salt can read a train whistle
by ear—the pitch, the tune, the duration declares
which conductor, what message, the urgency.

At the first of Hess' five sharp whistle blasts
we know in our very bodies that danger
is upon us.

The conductor and I spring in unison
from our chairs, me without even grabbing my hat,
then fly at a great lick down the tower's stairs.

One glance up the hillside reveals a rickrack wall
of timber, rooftops, Lord knows what else,
gathering up everything in its path.

I bolt across four sets of tracks and up the stairs
of the coal tipple. The water's roar joined with that
mournful whistle shriek—my ears still ring with it.

The dam that threatened year after year has failed
in spectacular fashion. Four more blasts before Hess
ties down his whistle—

a scream anyone within earshot can decipher.
Within minutes the wave uproots the entire tower.
(I look away when it goes under.)

Later I find among the debris my telegraph key,
that old vacuum brewer, and the faithful depot clock,
once affixed atop the tower like a full moon.
Its hands stopped cold at 3:08.

The Drifter

> Morgue Entry: *Male. 30 years. ... Open faced silver watch. 1 knife. 1 rule. 1 toothbrush. 1 lead pencil. Book of rates E.L.A.S. 1000 miles pass book.*

Here's the design: hop the Pennsylvania line
at East Conemaugh then on upstate to the Erie-New
York, all the way into St. Louis, change to the Frisco.
West, where the outlook opens wide: blue skies, sea-
washed air.

Yes sir, the Iron Horse, my way out of this smoke-
choked town. Sick to death of my skin crawling
with dust; crunching soot in my sleep.

Anyways, no job, no family; nothin' here
to root me. I'm carrying everything a fella needs
to strike out—my father's silver timepiece,
valuable as my thousand-mile pass—good as gold
in my pocket.

A knife, of course. What man worth his whiskers
doesn't carry some sort of blade? A rule, a pencil, a
book of rates. How many hot meals, tobacco plugs,
shoe shines, miles. Got it figured. Exacting, down to
the eighth inch, the last copper—that's me.

Rain still lashing this morning like a coachwhip.
A dark mist arcing over the hill, like some fine black
powder spewing straight out the ground. Best hightail it
toward the station.

What now! That ear-splitting thunder,
some fearsome rumble
booming down the mountainside?

In This Final Spinning Minute

>Morgue Entry: *Male. Red moustache. Open faced silver watch. Congress gaiters. Bunch of keys.*

Inside the steady pummel
of rain, its dogged tom-tom
against roof, against windows—
a growing rumble.

I step outside my door and directly
outside my body, into the storm's
ragged teeth. One foot slides
off earth's slippery edge.

Not the gathering wave so much
as the black mist moving
before it. Flock of obsidian,
explosion of crystals.

No: coal soot. Yes: A wash of ash
over the colossal wall of water.
The mine's raw tonnage
blown sky-high.

Cinders like a flight of souls
above the freighted swell. I crouch
into the howl of wind just outside
my swinging, half-hinged door.

Gouged into that wave (can I trust
my eyes?) train cars, cows, chimneys.
Breathless ticks before the wreckage
roars toward me …

I feel my mouth moving without
sound, shaping God's every name.
An upsurge bellow. The under-
world whirls street level.

Splintering of pillar, porch, frame
(I press my ears closed) closer now
to where I stand suspended
body and breath.

I feel nothing. Not even my feet
grazing the pavement
as the tidal maw draws me
                              into

Waterwheel

—Johnstown, PA. July 19, 1977

I heard my father's story a full two days later
after frantic calls home. All wires down.
Red Cross lines besieged. *Try again later ...*
                                                later.

On his way to work at the mill that morning,
my father's car headed down into the city
as the flood rose to meet him, rising fast, up

the steep road so that he threw the car into reverse
and sped some one thousand feet back up that incline,
shimmying curb-to-curb all the way to the house

on Bluff Street where he woke my mother, and together
they ran to the corner, Mom still in her bathrobe, to witness
the neighborhood below become a fast-running creek.

From a collision of thunder up near Erie, a series of storms
had followed one another like train cars on a track
moving down to the Conemaugh Valley,

opening their colossal cargo of rain over our town,
bursting dams that checked the river, washing away houses,
lives. Seventy-eight souls.

Through the years he'd tell it exactly the same way,
like a passage he'd memorized for school, with the same
wide-eyed astonishment as if he were once again

watching that torrent rush toward him—trapped
behind the wheel with no option but to hightail it
backward to higher ground.

Through the years I'd ask, *Tell me again, Dad, how you escaped
the flood that day*, and silently recite the story along with him,
like a prayer, and together we'd see the sky as a sheet
of molten steel, and the marvel of that surging tide.

II.

WAVE

I meet myself
as downpour—
my return
from the sky; hour
after endless hour
over the mountain lake
as self
amplifies self
and plummets.

Hettie Ogle, Western Union Telegraph Operator

> *This is my last telegraph. ...*
> —Hettie Ogle, Johnstown, 3:15 p.m., May 31, 1889
>
> Morgue Entry: ... *light brown hair, curly. Height 5'2". No upper teeth. ... Clothing all torn from body. Many who have seen the body think it to be that of Sister H. M. Ogle, Western Telegraph operator.*

Early to my station to sound the river:
by 7:40 the Conemaugh up fourteen feet.
Busy with my ticker all morning—

flooding, danger, prayed the town heed the warnings.

How could I have slept, dreamt of anything
but water, waves—the river rising surely
another full fathom through the night.

Relentless, this storm. The city had been living
beneath a waterfall; we did, this time, go under.

Three hours passed while six more feet
filled the channel. Still, the rain persisted.
It found me equally willful.

By noon, the depth gauge swept off;
waters climbing above floor level.
Beyond measure.

I hastened my girls, my instruments,
upstairs. Quickly! Tick on!

By 3:15, ground wires pulled, mid-
sentence, into the surge. The dam had
assuredly burst, and I am now washed

clear beneath the Lincoln Bridge—so very far
from my earthly work.

The Scullery Maid

> Morgue Entry: *Female age 35 to 40. Fair complexion. Large nose. Tall and strangely built. ... Working woman. Hands creased— evidently worked about a stove or cooking.*

When sails appeared like seraphim on the mountain lake, gliding against the dark pine ridge, I let myself be lifted into that vision.

In between basting and boiling, scouring, and mopping, I'd lean against the back-porch rail of the St. Charles Hotel and gaze up to the hills,

imagine myself as one of those fancy Clubhouse ladies with starched petticoats, a smart bonnet trimmed with bows and flowers, a wide silk ribbon tied 'neath my chin.

My hands would be smooth as the marble Virgin's at St. John's; not these rough, puckered mitts that know only boil, pluck, and scrub day in and out.

I'd be handed into a boat fitted with wings, white wings, stretched out like a sea bird, and float right off the mountain.

Oh, such fantasies! Until old Mr. Fitzharris hollers, on the regular, to get back to the kitchen.

By 11:00 that morning, water in the streets already head-high; no time to take up the rugs—I was swept up the stairs with all creation, jamming and shouting, *The torrent, the failed dam!* when the wave crashed the roof, hurled me back down and down; claimed me, dreams and all.

They found me in the cellar two days later, floating among jars of peaches and beans. My white underskirt flared about my body.

The Bookseller

> Morgue Entry: *package of photographs, large key, fountain pen, gold watch, tape measure, two pocket knives.*

That morning, like all others, I slipped down Main Street
to the Merchant Hotel at eight for my usual breakfast
before opening the shop, ten o'clock sharp.

Traffic at the shop the morning after Decoration Day,
given the town's exuberant mood, was bound to be brisk.

A steady rain had rinsed parade dust from the air,
inducing me to step out to the hotel porch
with my last cup of coffee and James' *Aspern Papers*.

Lulled by the strum of rain on the awning and absorbed
in my novel, I must have been caught unaware when the flood—
an actual wave!—advanced directly toward the hotel.

Swift, immense, a sheer wall of water spewing a vile spray
of black vapor, and bearing the most astounding array of items—
shingles, bricks, boards, cook stove, a coach.

Can I really have seen bodies joined to this mountain
of dark water? At first an upsurge bellow, like the basso
of an approaching train; then an engine rumble
as the wave rose, paused a long instant, midair

while the world hovered in a vacuum of sound,
of all sense until the balcony holding me in suspense
crashed to the ground, four stories below.

And now here I somehow stand, the book splayed open
against my chest. A coating of plaster and mud
smear my houndstooth suit and cake in my hair.

Wire-rim glasses askew. My jaw agape
in everlasting shock.

A Pool of Tears

Morgue Entry: *Female. Age 10 years. Blue cambric dress. Woolen skirt. Woolen stockings. Button shoes. Dark hair.*

"I wish I hadn't cried so much!" said Alice, as she swam about, trying to find her way out. "I shall be punished for it now, I suppose, by being drowned in my own tears!"
—Lewis Carroll, *Alice in Wonderland*

Only a very small wrong, I thought, unraveling
the bobbins in Mother's sewing basket, but the threads
were pretty spread across the floor, and in all this
awful rain the colors so cheerful.

After my scolding, I must have cried myself to sleep
and now wade down the stairs, hungry for a snack,
but wonder if I may be still in my bed, only dreaming
that water is filling my shoes, rising to my knees,

soaking my skirts with each step down into the parlor.
But I must be awake for the water is so cold and mucky,
and I'm shivering, calling for Mother. Has she floated
away; surely, she would not leave without me!

I'm swept into the parlor where all sorts of odd things
float about—a stew pot and pictures and chairs, and now
down the hallway, the upright comes thumping a waterlogged tune, followed by the bench spilling sheet music.

Oh, it's all too dreadful! It seems my tears have flooded
the house, and now the water is rising clear to my chin.
I must keep treading, but my arms are so tired.
Here's a chair leg I'll hold on to till father comes home.

But how will he ever get in? And now a swell
has carried me through to the pantry,
where rhubarb and oranges go bobbing;
maybe our house has tumbled into the sea.

If I could just reach the biscuit tin, I might grow bigger
and see my feet again. Look! There's the shore and a dodo,
holding out my thimble in his strange bird hand, and
beside him Mother with her sewing basket, beckoning.

The Lost Children

—(an erasure)

A few years,
wisp of fog
in the grass.

An hour
of music,
a cup of tears.

Miss Elizabeth Bryan

> Morgue Entry: *Age about seventeen. Of Germantown, Philadelphia. Brown dress. Bracelets, seven strands and locket with initials, "E. M. B."*

How wildly the scene outside my coach window
transformed as the Day Express swept
into Conemaugh Valley—rough Allegheny greens
descended to rain-guttered foothills.

A world utterly awash.

The steady beat—drumming of God's awesome fingers—
atop the wooden coach those five long hours
on the tracks while we awaited word: advance
or retreat.

My dear companion, Miss Paulson, lost
in her novel, even drifting off time to time.
Perhaps the wedding's gaiety of only a day before
suffused her dreams while this tireless storm,
this foreboding, filled my outlook.

But for some misshapen notion of comfort,
I might have survived! I turned back
for my overshoes in those seconds that I might have
leapt from the car,

ascended to higher ground, arm in arm with my friend.

What a story we would have recounted
down the years: how the wave simply lifted the train
off the tracks, tossed it into the swirl as easily
as one would pick up a cup, drop it in dishwater.

And how we cleared the great churn in the very nick of time.

This very night I might have settled
in my armchair—a book, a lively fire, children abed,
shoes kicked off by the hassock, embers
in their late-day chatter, and feeling nothing
but grateful.

The Carpenter

> Morgue Entry: *Male. Age 45. Height 6 ft. Very powerful man. Sandy hair. ... Bullet head. Massive jaws. On his right arm was tattooed a ballet dancer with a tambourine in her hand. Knees callused as though he worked at measuring. Expression indicated Irish nativity.*

My life was hoist, measure, pound. Making houses sturdy as myself, houses for the big bugs along Washington Street—the jewelers and bankers. Nothing but the best for that breed: braced framing, concrete slab, walls plumb as plumb is plumb.

So much a body reveals: my roughed-up knees read *measure*, feet bare and pocked announced hobnail shoes. Those shoes swallowed up by the flux and filth. My jaw, square as a four-walled room. Beale figured it right—my hands were indeed a fighter's. Any man, hey, I could thump him flat as a thick-shank nail.

But this torrent! A roil of saw logs, brick, axles, cattle, and swine. Christ-a-mighty! The whole hillside come down upon us like all wrath. They found me wedged in a stone foundation of a house I set right. For all my mass, I was no match for that water's brawn, its gnarled fist.

Sacramental

Water—
the spring-fed pond
where I swam all summer.
Every dip a baptism.
Renewed.

Deluged—
the wave-shattered town.
We clung to the railings.
Swept downstream.
Last rites.

The Dressmaker

Morgue Entry: *Foot of female. High button shoe. Black merino stocking.*

I.

Decoration Day the rain at last abated.
The washed air fairly glistened off drum rims, and
flags flew vivid blues and reds along Main,
where a multitude from far as Ebensburg,
come by special trains, had gathered.

Stores closed. School children released.
Cheers and laughter trilled with piccolos;
the whole town up-tempo
as the parade advanced.

Oh, it was grand! And I, spruced out
in my best shirtwaist, the indigo gingham
whose sleeves I yoked and edged
with ruffles.

Nothing so fine as the better ladies' dresses
I sewed—rustling folds of silk, velvet cloaks
fit for the opera house—but special enough
for holidays.

Poking from below my skirt hem,
the fancy tips of my new kid-leather
side-button boots—a month's worth
of sewing wages.

Stored in their leatherette box,
rubbed with Vaseline after each wear
and spared for occasions
such as this.

I loved that neat heel click
on the pavement, Sunday walks
through the park; their sharp tap
across the library's chestnut planks.

That sound grounded me
to the earth, announced my existence
in a crowd and bespoke an elegance
I would otherwise never own.

II.

O! Had I been left
all of a piece!

Of all the possessions on my person
that might have distinguished me
from the other morgue remains—
thimble, locket, door key, button hook—
that they should have found
only my high-button boot.

Just the one.

A scrap of black wool stocking
limp over the top.

My foot cushioned there
within its kid-lined recess.

To turn a pair of kid shoes

the goat's skin must be removed
before heat leaves
        its body, before

the pelt is brine-cured then
soaked six days in a drum,
        after which treated

with milk of lime; no lingering
protein, grease, or fat
        to sour the hide.

Unhaired and scudded next, best
with a dull knife; leave no trace
        of beast.

Pickled then, curried and finished
with dyes and polishes—
        no blemish.

Welt-stitched and snugly foxed—
leather stripping to secure the seam
        where sole meets upper.

The shoe supple now as
waterspill through blades
        of a wheel.

Little Shaver

> Morgue Entry: *Male, Nine years old. Black hair. Short pants with small bottle in pocket. Watch. Hatchet. Lead pencil. Shoe buttoner.*

On the doorstep of my ninth summer, I was
all hepped up from the Decoration Day parade—
the reed band, prancing horses, flags, a fleet
of steam cars puffing their glory into the crowd.

Later it rained and rained like God
was wringing out his laundry over the town.
I didn't mind the rising water—not at first.
It was like living on a creek bed.

I caught all manner of squiggly fellow
in the hair-tonic bottle Pop gave me,
and copied their shapes in my notebook.
Thought I'd maybe discover something new.

Mom cautioned about straying far
from the yard, with the creek flowing over,
but Sam and Henry was heading up
to the old wooden bridge across Toby Creek—

keeping tabs on the storm. We leaned over the rail,
howling into the roar of water getting higher
and higher, flowing at full chisel 'til
it snatched us right up and dumped us in the swirl.

We landed on a pile of timber washed down
from the yard up at Mineral Point and
went flying! It was the wildest ride I ever been on,
like a fantasy not even Jules Verne could dream up:

houses turned inside out with tables and cook stoves
and windows spinnin', and rooftops rushin' by
with people riding them, hanging on
to chimneys, shouting, reaching out their hands.

For a time, I thought I was having some wild dream,
and wanted so bad to please wake up. They found me
barefoot and staggered lookin', washed up in a garden,
Pale and delicate as a gardenia, some lady said.

Well, I never thought of myself as no flower
but am grateful she thought tenderly of me.
My bottle and lead pencil they found in one pocket,
my new shoe buttoner in the other.

The Season of Water

> Morgue Entry: *Female, white, Age twenty-six. Weight 125. Black ear drops. Two black hair pins. Gray skirt with red stripe. Blue stockings. Black button shoes. Medal and "Agnus Dei" around neck.*

We lived in a stone house in the vee of the mountains.
My James built our home from local sandstone;
best mason in County Galway. So, of course.
A grand home of our own making. Nor were we wanting
a place with ghosts about; other people's memories.

All that remains is the chimney, the very heart
of the house. Every stone tight to its mortar. Imagine
water overpowering stone walls, and then
sparing the hearth. Come to that, imagine a surge
of water sweeping away a town and its people.

Between crops and politics, there was no staying in Ireland.
Even twenty years after the famine, folks still going hungry.
We took a steamer to the States, and made our way
to Johnstown, a place all a-bustle with foundries and mills,
where any man with skill could find work. Immigrants
like us nattering together in their native tongues. Like us,
digging new roots.

The Alleghenies rimmed our view; hogback ridges
the shades and shadows of green, almost
like home. And then the lake shimmering up there—
mirage. I was given to think it was the water sprites
making it gleam so.

Mutterings in town about the high-falutin' up
at the clubhouse taking their leisure on the
mountain lake. We keep the wheels oiled
and turning, and they rake in the profits.

But this talk of unionizing—I'd be dog wide of it!
We've a proper roof, and lie down at night
with our bellies satisfied. All that matters.

Mutterings, too, this spring of that lake
not proper cared for and ready to burst.
What with all these storms. Just talk,
our neighbors said. Needless to worry.
So, we didn't.

Then came the season of water. A bit of flooding
every year, situated as we were, but nothing
like that spring of 1889. The longest stretch
of wet in memory. I hadn't thought it possible
to live in a country more drenched than Ireland.

Lordy, if it wasn't storming, it was snowing. Clear into May.
And then the snowmelt down that mountain, tumbling
into rivers and creeks. Out into the streets. It was like living
at the bottom of a well with the rope bucket not scooping out
but pouring in.

The poor horse, his feet waterlogged; shoes
sucked right off in the mud. Nearly lame.
His sweet temperament turned dark as the skies.

We darted and dashed here to there and back,
our clothes never drying entirely. Mildew and mud
in the air, moldered in every corner.

Water filled my dreams, and I'd startle awake
with a gasp. Damp and still shivering in our woolen
stockings and flannel shirts. Only our bodies
to keep each other warm.

When the sun did show itself, the sky was sooty
like a dirty old sheet flung up over our heads.
Factory fumes smudged the clouds and hung
like a dark wolf over the setting sun.

Even still, most days I was glad to be gone from a country on its knees. Glad for James' regular wages. Other days, when the river ran under my door, given the thirty-dollar fare for a ticket in steerage, I might have gone back. Ha! Easy enough to say now, after the flood. Everything now is *after*—a line drawn in the muck.

The Blue Door

—(an erasure)

Through the deepest end,
    its liquid abandon, our selves
      sink
          rise.

We encounter new bodies
in murmurs
          of water.
The drowning
    we have to do.

Water sends us through
the blue door.

Holding tight
to the edge
    we
      breathe   and
          let
      go.

Next to me

at the flood museum, a young girl presses a button
on the diorama again, and again the mountain lake overflows
the dam, masses, and rushes down the winding spine
of the Conemaugh Valley.

She scurries to keep pace with the blinking lights
along the length of the glass case as together we watch
the water gather, surge, crash into the miniature city.

She skips back and reaches again for the button, giggling
louder than the voice of the disembodied narrator.
But in my head only echoes of the wave's roar, smash
of bricks and beams, shingles ripping. Screams. Silence.

This old stone building was once a library,
my childhood haven. Weathered spines held the promise
of some incredible elsewhere while the heady blend
of Pine-Sol and inked vellum in the shushed reading room
instilled the thrall of story, character, outcome.

Now I've returned to sift through artifacts—
a pair of wire spectacles (what books were read
through these lenses?), a once-white cotton glove
(folded into the other at church?), a ceramic doll.
Stained, disjointed (what of the child who loved her?)

As I handle the slight heft of each, the lure of story
draws me in. Sorting through boxes of musty letters
and photos, I search for a way to tell the tale of how
a doll in gingham came to rest in a small pine box
in the back room of a museum.

III.

CARRY

Only so much I can collect
before my body becomes reliquary.
Crucifix, brick, trolley coin, serving spoon,
old men, children. I gather all
forged of tin or flesh, in sheets of silt
and ruin.

After two days I return

to dig through debris, the house
heeled over. Broken. I stumble
over a table leg. Curse a blue streak.
The aproned ladies shake their heads,
try to tempt me away with ham and biscuits.

Emily. Somewhere in this wreck.
I dare not leave.

I climb again and again
to the second-floor landing.
Two steps at once. Will never stop
climbing or hearing the deep rip.
Wall from frame. Crack and crash
in the street, like ships against rocks.

I still feel her hand closed in mine
as I pull her. Still, I am pulling her.
Her grasp slips. I turn to see her,
over and over see her lose her footing.
A tangle of skirts. The river-slimed stairs.

The vision of dark water swirling.
Transom-high. Em's face a porcelain mask.
Her mouth astonished—a wild soundless terror.
And her gasp.

A thousand times I've turned and watched her
go under. A thousand times I did not save her.
Could not save her—water fast at my heels.
Sucking at my shoes, my pant legs. *Listen!*
Her voice under the stair.

Is my mind playing tricks?   Can it be?
Look   just there   in the pool beneath the stair
Her teacup   yes!   in pieces   and   there
her sleeve   Em!

Now a voice *It's just a rag, don't you see.*
A touch on my arm. *Lay down that shovel,
poor man. Come with me.*

Dear Father,

June 3, 1889

Since arriving in Johnstown, I have been knee-deep in filth. Nothing could have prepared me for the sights I have witnessed: carcasses and all manner of objects—locomotive cars, stew pots, shoes strewn about in the mud and gravel. The dead animals, some in the streets but mostly along the riverbanks, are a most disturbing sight.

A good supply of rosin and tar has been indispensable for cremating the poor beasts. Everywhere scattered are small fires for the burning of mattresses, garments, carpets, and the like fouled by the floodwaters. Mercifully, however, the weather has turned cool, slowing the molder.

John, another supervisor, says that our clothing best be incinerated when we have finished our duties here, as no laundry soap could remove the rot of this work. I wonder if I, myself, will ever feel clean again. A good scrubbing with three bars of lye might do the job. I may have to lather the inside of my nose, as well, to get rid of the stench!

It all strikes me as a scene from Ambrose Bierce—those ghastly stories you admire. Ruin fully imagined. Most houses have been taken down to jagged splinters, like wooden crates, open to the elements. Those left standing teem with debris and filth. John says better that they had been swept away, too, and I can't argue that.

The cellars are by far the worst—muddy pits of decay of every imaginable sort. This is where my responsibility in the Sanitary Corps lies: directing teams of men to disinfect before excavation, and then again afterward. Just yesterday we waded into a hotel basement to discover a young woman floating among canned preserves. The look of terror on her face I shall never forget. As far as I know, no one's yet claimed her. A serving girl, most likely.

My crew and I go house to house. If you could just see the children's faces: little wraiths, smeared, bewildered, and eerily quiet, as if their spirits have slipped away. I think many have lost a parent or siblings. Many on the verge of pneumonia, or the typhus that has started to spread. It just about breaks my heart.

There are scarce practical items to hand. We want for the simplest things—dishes, a comb, dry socks, a clean spoon. We had no vessel for dissolving the copperas, that vile-smelling disinfectant, and resorted to climbing into a wrecked store for tin pots and a wash boiler. If Mother and the neighborhood ladies in the community want to help, perhaps they could gather some basic provisions and send them through. How glad I am that I thought to pack paper and a pen. I only hope mail will go through to Pittsburgh.

We're told that Miss Clara Barton will arrive soon. She is said to be a small engine of efficiency. We expect she'll bring in those items to keep the citizens clean, dry, nourished, and sane. I do not know how people are carrying on after the shock of losing all earthly possessions. And on top of that, their loved ones. Some families have been wiped out entirely. Oh, and I have not had any news of Philip Anderson, but am continuing my inquiries. So many have gone missing in the flood. I hope to have good news to pass along to your neighbor.

I do not mean to go on in a complaining manner, Father, but it helps me immensely to unburden myself, and to set down a record of what I have witnessed here. Tell me, has Elizabeth had her baby yet? I'm anxious to know which I'll have, a new niece or a nephew. Grand either way!

I feel that once I am back in my warm and tidy home with Madeleine and the children, this shall all fade like a strange dream. I shall spare her the distress of my conditions as she is burdened enough with managing the household alone, and so easily given to worry. I trust that you will not share the details of my news with her. I miss her enormously but shan't allow myself to dwell on all I must presently live without.

I have gone on long enough and should finish now before daylight fades completely. We have been housed in large tents, hardly homey, but adequate. My cot is a mean, squeaky thing, too short for my height, but honestly, I am so weary in mind and body when I lie down that sleep overtakes me before my head finds the pillow.

Please give my love and a peck on the cheek to Mother. Tell her I shall savor her Sunday dinners so much the more when I return. Keep this city and its people in your prayers.

Your loving son,

William

Colonel Unger, Returning to the Clubhouse

> *Oh, it seemed to me as if all the destructive elements of the Creator had been turned loose at once in that awful current of water.*
> —Colonel Elias J. Unger, president of the South Fork Fishing and Hunting Club

Wind sighs across the crater that held
Lake Conemaugh. I look away, up
to the Allegheny ridges, and imagine
wind-driven white sails, the easy glide
of boats, and almost hear the rise and fall
of light chatter, laughter across the water,
and the *plash* of bobbins striking the surface.

Quiet now, but for that eerie wind, like
a muffled hum of lost voices. The thunderous
water—a full twenty million tons of pent-up water—
breaching the dam resounds in my head.
I cannot close my eyes but see
that rush of water, everything moving
but standing still. I step outside
my very body; the air itself charged
with disbelief.

Engineer Fulton's words echo, too:
... the want of a discharge pipe ...
destructive leaks ... only a question of time ...
impossible to estimate how disastrous
this flood would be.

Warnings I chose to dismiss.

Year after year the dam had held
against heavy rain. I believed
it always would. That it must.
That providence could not be so cruel.

When I look out upon what is left of the lake—
a puny meander of water in the mud-bottom ooze,
flailing of scattered trout in the shallow channels—
and to the valley below, stripped, desolate
as a barren planet, I wish to Christ I had been
downstream of that wave.

Clara Barton
at Her Dressing Table

—Washington, D.C., June 5, 1889

The old woman in the oval mirror stares back at me,
perched at my vanity in cotton chemise and underskirt.
Never mind the lines crisscrossing my face; all that matters
is the work yet to do.

Still a full hour before I depart for Pennsylvania—
time enough to make myself presentable, finish packing
my hand luggage for the train trip from Washington
to Johnstown, a city overcome by flood
just five days past.

I've set aside my day skirt and waist in the wardrobe,
and draped my corset and cover over the wooden chair.
My tapestry bag readied—journal and cedar pencil,
handkerchief, fan, coins for tipping the porters.

Obligatory hat and gloves placed at the foot
of the boardinghouse bed; doubtless they'll remain
on a bedpost or peg once I arrive.

If I were to lend credence to the astonishing headlines—
Town Is Wiped Entirely Off the Map; 12,000 to 15,000 dead!
Hundreds of Corpses Floating Down the Conemaugh; and
most horrific of the lot, *Two Thousand Burn to Death*
In the Wreck—I would be daunted by the task awaiting me.

Newsmen what they are, the actual numbers will likely
be less than half what's in print. I straighten my spine
and take a long breath. After Antietam, I believe myself
equal to anything.

My long brown hair a shade darker now; I detect glints
of iron gray in the mirror. Still thick and fine, though, falling
in waves down my back. My "crowning glory," Mother would say.
Otherwise, the glass has verified throughout these 67 years
that I am plain, which suits my practical nature.

With the routine fifty brush strokes I begin the calculations
of supplies, quantities thereof, delivery method …
14, 15: coal tar, matches … 21, 22: muslin, borax …
35, 36: water, lumber … 49, 50: a team of doctors, nurses.

A simple hair dressing this morning: parted
straight down the center into equal panels
with the wooden comb, then plaiting in back,
and coiled into a bun. A quick twist of the sides
into rope braids, then wound back around. Done.

One by one, I pick five hairpins from the old rouge pot;
weave them into the compact knot of hair, and with each pin
list another item: *soap, cook pots, blankets, clothing, linens.*
A quick crimping around the part to shadow the roots, then
pat every last hair into place.

On an ordinary morning, I would have run hair oil
through the length, taken the time to fashion English braids,
and secured the whole of it with a tortoise shell comb.
But this is not an ordinary morning.

A deep breath then before rising to dress: first opening
the corset lacings and wrapping it around my middle.
Fastening the busk, I stand taller than my five feet.
Reaching back, I snug the tie loops tight. Then once again,
tighter.

Flood and Fire

—(a remix)

Along the gray, spent sky
whips an unchimneyed wind
whistling thick and rude.

Town-caught flame,
the white riot of trees
here, there.

Unfamiliar now
the homeliest things—
a cup, a chair.

Once the Floodwaters Recede

—after Ezra Pound's "In a Station of the Metro"

Searching through splintered remains of the
house, I saw her at the window, an apparition
surely, but seeming so real—the figure of
Abigail, flawless in her green silk, gazing through the
panes of a window, since shattered. I've studied the faces
of women in tatters passing on the streets in
this shell of a city; hunted through churches, houses, by the
river, hoping to catch her in the bewildered crowd.

I find her wedding pearls, slipped from their strand like petals
of our dogwood in blossom; the shining gems scattered on
the muddied rug. As I gather them in my hand, I'm struck by a
knowing—my search is done. Oh, dreary world, a vision of wet
bare trees out of season—so many sad figures clad in black.
The storm in its fury has torn all brilliance from the bough.

The Saints Have Faces of Stone

I kneel at the font in this church-turned-morgue
before entering the nave without husband and daughter.

People file by rows of bodies as though in a fog,
down the long aisles of this church-turned-morgue.

My gloved hand shakes, checking once more this coffin-lid tag
listing gold band, cuff buttons, silver watch—all so familiar.

And there, beside Robert in this church-turned-morgue,
asleep in her gingham dress, the small body of our daughter.

Tired   I walk toward everything

> —*Clara Barton, stepping from the train after*
> *The Great Flood in Johnstown, June 5, 1889*

except fear
for fear has no place among mud-shrouded
bodies—livestock, people—whole

and pieced along the riverbanks.
Houses, once upright shelters, folded in
upon themselves; hearths now open

to the drizzle: cook stove here, table
leg, crockery there. Foundation stones,
chimney bricks everywhere.

Almost underfoot, a porcelain doll: blue
broadcloth dress, white apron, smeared.
Jointed limbs intact. I place her in my coat pocket.

Skeins of wire stab the air.
Splintered timbers, engines and steel rail
mangled in this prodigious mix.

The dazed search through the rubble for a familiar.
Oh, I have seen the likes on battlefields—the aftermath
of soldiers outfitted and ready,

but here is a town wholly unarmed, shadowed
by an enemy proclaiming,
I am the modern Morpheus,
a wild beast,
a paroxysm of rage.

In this wasteland fear will press its sway.
Stronger yet is necessity, as ever I've seen.

Ballad of the Makeshift Morgue

> —*The Millville School House, turned morgue, was one of the few buildings remaining on its foundation after the flood.*

Dear lady, pass this way with me.
Step carefully down the rows
of coffined victims—some maimed or burnt.
Shhhh; only his face will show.

We'll read the tag on each box lid,
which tells what may distinguish
your husband from another chap:
old scar, a ring, a mustache.

Now bear in mind that might be all
to signify the person
who lies within a rough pine box—
what's left past recognition.

This school once hummed with minds a-brim;
John Keats and long division.
Still on the chalkboard rests the dust
of rhyme scheme; decimal precision.

Now bodies stretch across the desks;
at peace or fair disfigured.
Swept downriver, pried from debris,
townsfolk fixed in rigor.

Benumbed by such a scene: take heart.
Just say what clothes, what weight,
for I'm the one who lays them out—
I'll know your man by sight.

Just now you blanch by this next box—
so cruel, your utmost fear!
Poor woman, take my handkerchief.
Let's get you some fresh air.

The Errant Husband

> Morgue Entry: *Male. Age forty-five. Weight 180. Height 5 feet 10 inches. White bunch of keys. $1.13 loose. White bone-handled knife.*

I shouldn't have left you
home by yourself—water
in the street

nearly reaching
our kitchen window; the gaslight
sputtering, but

Darling, so little
money, and end
of the month—rent, the gas bill,

our anniversary. You must
understand; third turn, an extra
shift, and you still dreaming. If only

I'd known
the mill would send us—
every last man—back home, and I,

God! in my unnerved state, stopped
by the saloon; just one
whiskey to steady

me; just the one. Then
there was old Hooper, outside calling:
Help me get this horse hitched!

That horse suddenly a-swirl in
the flooded street, jack-knifing Hoop's
buggy; all a-frenzy. Caught

beneath those buggy wheels, it
had nothing to do
with the drink—all the wreckage

in the water knocked me
under, and now
your measured footfall

near this shoddy casket ... that you some-
how survived and now
come lookin' for me in this God-

forsaken place, a schoolhouse
defiled, and children
coffined here, too.

In spite of
all
my folly, you come: beyond

bearing even
in this nether state.
Pass me by now,

dear Anna, for
they could not loosen
the grimace

from my face; you'll never
know the last word on my lips
was your name.

Attempting to Speak of Home

—(an erasure)

Thundercrack
in a jagged flash
the mystery of shoes
filled with water.

Homesick, the dark breath,
the open wound.

The wind licks
the body's wounds. Animal
darkness in the blink
of an eye.

The stone's inscription
in place of home.

Child, pushing against
the horizon, already voiceless
exhaling waves
of longing.

Child, the seedpod
of your dreams heavy.
Motherground stunned.

Driven from home,
wind-whipped and weeping
in the cave of the mouth.

If a language sounds
like a mare's whinny or
a blackbird, a gnashing
from afar, a stranger has
his homeland in his arms.

Pray for home, heart
in earth cinders.
O Soul, lead
to hearths of rest.

The Poison of Her Mourning

> *Many a woman has been laid in her coffin by the wearing of crape.*
> —The Dietetic and Hygienic Gazette, 1898

She can guess the contents of the parcel
from her widowed aunt. She runs her hand
across the gusseted paper and hears the rasp
of crape, feels the crimped outline of a bonnet's brim.
The garments' pleating, stiff as wooden rules,
indent her fingers.

She holds the package out in both hands, tottering
under its weight, and sinks to the edge of the bed.
Between layers of white tissue, three jet-black dresses:
one of poplin, one taffeta, and the last a satin.

One by one, she holds them against her body. Wide,
like her aunt, but she will fit them to her shape.
And each one dull in the morning light. The cloth
as muted as a life newly halved.

For the full year and one day of deep mourning,
she will reflect no light; become a shadow
thrown at noon, passed without notice on the street.

Between the dresses she finds a silk pouch, knotted and tied
with black ribbon. Inside, her grandmother's lusterless
black pearls, cool and dry as a coiled snake in her palm.
She remembers the old lady's severe appearance,
like a silhouette in motion, after her grandfather died.

The hair on the back of her neck would rise
when the silent, dismal figure rustled into the room.
She sighs to think of her solemn inheritance, and that now
even her jewelry must signify absence.

The last and gloomiest, the weeping veil—byzantine web
of gauze, double-layered, longer than she is tall, and lead-
weighted at its silken hem. She tacks it to the bonnet, and sets it
with effort on her head.

She turns toward her vanity, pushing aside the cloth
covering the mirror, and regards her reflection
with a shudder. One week widowed, and she has become
a specter, or worse, a nun.

True, she is grateful—these fabrics too dear for what
he has left her, the accounts she must somehow live inside.
His saloon might miss him more. It was his place of refuge
every ordinary morning after a long night turn at the Iron Works,
and even that day flooding destroyed the city.

By noon, a channel of water was at sloshing level
with her parlor window. She paced, waiting for him
to return, feeling more frightened and more alone
by the minute. His drinking had been her grief.
His death brought a new, attenuated sorrow.

Out of doors, she'll don garments of aniline black,
the darkest mourning hue made from a mordant
of coal tar, copper chloride, and arsenic. The dye
seeps in the rain, and in the dampness of sweat.

In time she'll learn to avoid the sun, to check
the turn of her head—even a breeze stirs the dye
in the draped folds that will discolor her skin,
sting her vision, short her breath.

Her breasts will sully; sooty rivulets mark her neck;
cheek abraded by the crape moving against it.
No cake of lye will touch it. She will scrub herself
raw with oxalic acid, cream of tartar, and still
be tarnished.

Throughout the long year, while she turns
through the market aisles or bends to the kneeler,
the garments' brush and rub will deepen the stain.
And with a gesture so simple as a sideways glance,
she will breathe in the poison of her mourning.

Summer along the Stonycreek

From a needle eye in the Alleghenies
this sheet of liquid shimmer
unseams the earth.

Steel rail and forest trail
run alongside, north and west
to the Laurel Highlands. At this bend
the current circles, chisels, deepens

for the child's cannonball,
the raccoon's cupped hands,
ribbon snake's undulations,
a polished assembly of stars.

See how the water gathers
oak's shadow, hemlock's needled brush
in its wending,

how the shifting clouds and lift
of broad-winged hawk echo
on its surface.

One with sky, river meets itself
as deluge, thin rain, as mist.

A body could float through time
on its muscled back. Our stories
are ferried in its depths: caravan
of arrowhead, latchkey, crockery, bone.

Listen now to the river's patter, reminding us
Not everything is broken.

IV.
FLOW

My mercy rests in quench, cleanse, nourish.
Mercy yet to claim a last breath as my own.
Undone apron, lace curtain—spectral in the surge.

When the tumult above recedes, sounding only
the hollow contralto of crows, sky mirrors
a broken stillness, and I discover a depthless peace.

After Ruin

—(a cento)

Sometimes I hear the earth's sunken voice,
    a throat-slit pouring silk, saying
        this is water; this is darkness;

this is a body fitting your description. Saying
    we can never be without loss
        too long.

The cemetery expands its borders—little milky crosses
    grow like teeth. I knew I would lose you. Why
        do stars break the morning sky?

I've engraved your name
    on the palms of my hands. We are two guests
        on an excess, fugitive cloud.

Some say we are living
    at the end of time. An afterlife
        of parts—rubble, but not without shape;

the sunset's patchy rust; a creek of shadows; a body
    displaced against the pull of the waters.
        No me, no you. No beginning, no end.

Come home, come home, the five porches weep.
    Old bone home—mottled mildewed wallpaper
        like a wet coat we couldn't put back on;

a naked animal in search of a pelt. Some things
    are hidden from us: the film of old water in a well,
        glaciers in a slow dissolve.

Eight weeks of deluge and gloom, but dear eager earth
    makes its impossible offer: one thousand birds in the hand,
        well water sweet for a hundred miles, and light,

more new light. How kind time is. Messages from the dead
arrive like calm white birds with a gift, and all
the sky there is fills my throat.

My Dearest Madeleine,

June 8, 1889

Can it be only a week since I left home? I still see you standing at the doorstep, wrapped in your blue shawl, the one that matches your eyes, waving goodbye and smiling so bravely. You are my plucky girl, managing the household and the children alone. I know you are equal to the task, and have nothing but admiration for your ability.

My work with the Sanitary Corps proceeds very well. The crews have cleared and cleaned the houses still standing, and we now concentrate on the public buildings. The Corps has been greatly tasked with cleaning up this city. I am heartened, Madeleine, by the community spirit. Supplies and food and volunteers from all our neighboring states. Yesterday a shipment of hams from Cincinnati! The commissary is well-stocked, and I am well-fed. For all this, I may return home sooner than expected. I'll look a little rougher for this work, but I hope that you will still let me into the house!

Miss Clara Barton arrived three days ago and has already set up hospital tents and shelters with running water. She passed by me in the street in a brisk rush just yesterday. I was taken with her small stature—she can't be above five feet. I hear that it's made up for by her large personality. All no-nonsense, with a mulish authority. She puts me in mind of your Aunt Peg. Efficient, but not the kind of woman who puts one at ease. Still and all, she sets her own needs no higher than any other's. She has set up her Red Cross headquarters in a boxcar. A crate for her desk. Imagine!

And how is your garden coming along, my dear? I imagine you've got the carrots, chard, and lettuce in. You had mentioned adding beets this year. Between you and my mother, we shall rival the green grocer!

My greatest want, of course, is home. Our warm and tidy home. Always the aroma of biscuits baking. Oh, to be there with you and Beth and Tommy. Your letters lift my spirits. I had to laugh at your description of Tommy climbing the maple during hide and seek, then having to announce his hiding spot because he couldn't get back down. That boy! How he manages to keep his limbs intact I do not know.

You will appreciate this story about a child named Gertrude Quinn, five years old, just like our Beth. She survived by holding fast to a mattress that carried her two miles downriver, until a stranger leapt into the water, and pulled himself up onto the mattress with her. He managed to toss her a good fifteen feet into the arms of a man leaning out of an open window. She was wrapped in a blanket and kept with a family until finally reunited with her poor father. He had given up hope of ever finding her, and when he learned she was alive, he raced to that home, shaving cream still covering half his face. Oh, my dear, it brings me to tears, the small miracles such as this.

You need not worry about my welfare, my love. I am fine, truly, but for missing you. Tonight, I will imagine your hand, cool on my forehead, your fingers in my hair, and a kiss to rest my spirit. I understand now why a soldier's most sacred possession is his beloved's portrait, carried in the pocket closest to his heart.

Keep well, dear girl. I shall write again soon. Kiss the children for me and pray for us all.

Your loving husband,

William

Clara Barton
Reports from the Field

—Johnstown, PA, September 9, 1889

Half my life has been spent in motion,
and so it is fitting I conduct my field work
from this abandoned boxcar. What do I need
beyond a wooden crate for a desk, milking stool
for a chair? My spine a sufficient backrest.

Three months now since The Great Flood,
and already we've built housing for scores
of homeless. Running water, both cold and hot.
No person in need of clothing or food is left
empty-handed.

Thanks to my nurses, the typhus is contained.
If only we could heal broken spirits. I trust
time will do its best work there. Never have I
been prouder to see Red Cross banners flying
above our white tents.

General Hastings has proved a worthy partner.
I recall our first meeting in June when, ankle-deep in muck,
hatless, doubtless disheveled, I stood surveying
the devastation, when he swung down from his horse,
and offered his hand: *Dear woman, may I assist you?*
I had to hide my smile.

At the end of a long day, I prize the night's silence.
Let the visions of wreckage, the bewildered faces
fall away. I stretch out on a cot narrow as myself,
and feel the fatigue in these old limbs.
Glad for clean bedding and a woolen blanket
this rainy night.

I shall not leave until my work here is finished.
Daily the town rebuilds, home by home,
shop by shop. Smoke from the Gautier Steel works
will rise again, like Lazarus, having nothing whatever
to do with miracles.

Out of Ruin

—Inspired by a photo collage by Matthew Wolfe

Our house still stood after the floodwaters receded, situated as we were on the hillside. The wave climbed only as high as the second story before it fell away, having swamped furniture, rugs, clothing, and swept the silver, the crockery, my papers. Our essentials. I can't imagine how the house itself was not carried off on the back of that enormous rush of water.

After the men and I cleared the mud and rot covering floors and walls, Margaret and I returned to see what might be salvaged. Room to room, she stifled a cry, holding my handkerchief to her mouth against the heavy river odor. Neither of us spoke what most troubled our minds: that we had lost all but the floorboards and frame. That is, until we ascended into the attic, where, remarkably, it was dry as bone, as if the space belonged to the clubhouse on the mountain, untouched by the flood.

And there, along the eaves, an odd assortment of items stacked for a rainy day's sorting. Volumes of Dickens in their red leather covers, Dad's old brass kaleidoscope, a tin of Greenbrier tobacco—why I saved it I don't know, for I no longer smoke, but my cousin, Joseph, whose house fell in entirely upon itself, would surely savor a plug of tobacco. I'll pocket the tin for him. Poor soul.

Margaret was astonished to find her mother's lacquered box, a pretty thing, nestled there among this hodgepodge. She let out a small gasp as she pulled it free and swung the latch aside. Inside was a brooch, a gold and silver piece in a coiled floral pattern. Slightly tarnished, clearly old, and clearly of great value to Margaret.

She ran a finger over the intricate design a long moment, then pinned the brooch to the collar of her dress. I'll never forget how my Margaret tipped her chin, the way she will when dogged on a topic, pulled back her shoulders and said, "We will begin again."

John Hess' Last Day

—East Conemaugh, 1906

The river still rises in my dreams,
and we fly down the tracks just ahead
of the wave that engulfed the city.

I race my engine, breakneck,
sounding that long whistle all the way,
then startle awake, sweated and elated—
somehow my crew survived!

My engine was later restored.
I never would have believed it possible,
after seeing her tumbled on her side
with the other cars, like a bunch
of dead cows.

After seventeen years, I close my eyes
to this sick room, and clear as my own
wife's face, remember—

> swinging up to the cab next to the fireman,
> checking the gauges and valves, seeing
> a good fire in the box, the gleam
> of the steel rail ahead. ...

I was one with that engine.
My hand on the throttle, feeling
the shudder of power beneath me;
steaming her down the line.

Now I hear a distant train's moan and chuff.
If only I could rise from this bed, walk
to the window, watch the white blast of steam,
the progress of engine, coach, caboose
like wind around the mountain bend.

Interview on the Ten-Year Anniversary of the Johnstown Flood

—May 31, 1899

Lordy, I don't much dwell on how we had to haul them bodies
out of the Conemaugh, but I remember it like it was yesterday.
Some sights never leave your mind, much as you'd like them to.

Well, the flood didn't leave much of my farm—shell of a house
and two milk cows left. My Guernseys, still in the barn, higher up
the hillside. Rest of the herd, mostly Jerseys, scattered in the field below.
Scared dumb by that rumble and big wave come down the mountain.
No way I could round them up quick. Not without me going under
with them. I can still picture that wave sweeping them belly up,
kicking and bawling.

So, I helped find the dead and bring them up from the river. However we could.
On doors, planks of wood—anything solid and flat enough to bear a body.
No wagons handy, so we hauled each one through the thick mud to the saloon.
Not for a drink, although I could-a used a stiff one. It was turned into a quick
set-up morgue, close to the stone bridge where the river caught fire.

Oh, mister, those cows. A pitiful thing. Moans humanlike when the water
washed over them. Never felt so damn helpless.

Well, the water hadn't receded all the way, so we waded right into that mess
of debris and carnage—that's not too strong a word to use for it. I threw
my dungarees in the bin right after. Never get the char and rot out of them.

Had a name for every one of them cows. And they'd come right to me
when I called them. Knew their names. Some sweeter than others, but all
of them good gals.

Okay, if you must know, I'll tell you about hauling the bodies. Can't say
trudging through that muck with water-swollen bodies didn't weigh down
these old legs. Think that's what did my knees in. I'd stop long enough
at the saloon morgue to catch my breath and got a glimpse of the undertakers
hosing the mire and scraping blood off bodies we brung, before they pushed
their sleeves back up to set about their terrible business.

I'm sure many a glass was raised to the poor souls in that saloon
once the world turned right-side-up. Not by me, though; I could never
walk in there again and see anything but death.

I'm thinking my cows likely felt it coming, the way animals are tied so tight
into nature, you know. They were restless all day. Lost a good dozen
quality milkers. Ah, well, nothing to do for it now.

I'll be deviled to know why you'd ask about the condition of the bodies.
Now I'd heard my Pap's war stories, but ain't nothing can match
what I witnessed down there at the bridge. People bloated, mangled,
in pieces, charred. What water and fire won't do to a body.

Suzie was my favorite Jersey. She had this soft brown fur. Really soft.
And the biggest, most beautiful eyes you'd ever like to see on an animal.

Right, well, those bodies, straight out of a horror story: one man's arms
tight around a beam, like he's still hanging on for dear life. Then springing back
around that shape once we pulled them free. Sprung up in the air like that
all the way to the morgue. Frightful.

Ladies, half-buried in mud. We had to dig them out. Some limp
as dish rags. Skirts pulled away by the water. I was ashamed to look,
to touch their bare legs when we pulled them loose and lifted them.
Only legs I'd ever seen or touched was my Alice's.

Alice loved the cows, too. We never had children, so we poured it out
on the animals. Not a thing most farmers would admit to, but
there you have it. Just as well Alice didn't live to see any of it.

You know, it's the faces I can't stop seeing. Lips twisted around what
might-a been their last words. Or hollers. I almost expected to hear
what they'd wanted to say upon leaving the world. Now, I won't
make too much mention of the children, so don't go asking about them.
Like cast-off rag dolls in the filthy water.

Christ. Puts a man in doubt about his maker's mercy. He ought to at least
let a person leave the world same way's they come into it. It's the pieces
stays with me most. So many feet. Just feet. Carts lined with them.
Still in their button shoes, like it was some kind of store display.
Like they might break into a jig. Now if that don't spoil your sleep,
I don't know what would.

Against Consolation

—(an erasure)

```
nothing           ash
         on the wind         so
   fine              undetected
             through stalks
       of grass
these first
             days
                     of spring
    no use
           now                   for a slender
      comb           thumbs
  things of
       this world       molecules
    whisper
             a modest life
```

I Washed into the World

I washed into the world on the sodden mattress
that floated my pregnant mother
into the second story window of Alma Hall.

In the pitch blackness of that shivering night,
I am told the contractions came on full force.
Her screams of pain likely drowned out

by the shouts and sobs of two-hundred-some
terrified and injured in that same room; by the wind's
sharp howl, the incessant crash and splinter
of buildings, bodies, God-knows-what outside.

Standing here now in front of Alma Hall, I gaze up
to the second-floor watermark, the elliptical arches
like raised eyebrows, and conjure some primal memory

of being delivered from one floating world
into another by a doctor with three broken ribs
while eighteen feet of water sloshed at the sill.

I am told that the Presbyterian Church steeple
split the wave in two, sending the wall of water
to either side of the hall, sparing all but one
of those sheltered inside.

Over the years I have pieced together
what I've been told about the night of my birth
when a flood leveled the city of Johnstown.
A patchwork of story and surmise.

On my fiftieth birthday, I've returned to see the lanterns
lit along the stone bridge, to visit the ground
where my ancestral home folded into itself
like an envelope

I have come to visit the plot of the unknown drowned
at Grandview Cemetery, and run my hand along the arc
of every blank stone.

END NOTES

The morgue entries were drawn from the original *Morgue Book of 1889*, where descriptions of the victims were recorded. Rev. David Beale was appointed Emergency Morgue Head after the flood, responsible for providing written descriptions of victims' features, clothing, and personal items for the purposes of identification. The morgue book is now archived by the U.S. National Park Service.

In "Getting the Message Through," the three uppercase messages are the quoted telegraph warnings sent down the valley by telegrapher Emma Ehrenfeld just before the South Fork Dam broke.

In "John Hess Ties the Engine Whistle Down," the italicized line is taken from Engineer Hess' sworn statement during an investigation by the Pennsylvania Railroad Company after the flood.

"The Lost Children" is an erasure from the poem "Tears," by Lizette Woodworth Reese.

"The Blue Door" is an erasure and title from the poem "The Blue Door," by Yoko Danno and James C. Hopkins.

"Next to me": The Cambria Public Library was rebuilt after the flood of 1889 demolished the original library. The new library was Andrew Carnegie's gift to the city after the flood, a gesture of recompense from one of the founders of the South Fork Fishing and Hunting Club whose membership neglected repairs of the manmade lake. The library was converted into the Johnstown Flood Museum in 1973.

"Flood and Fire" is a remix from the poem "Spicewood," by Lizette Woodworth Reese.

"Once the Floodwaters Recede" is a golden shovel from the poem "In a Station of the Metro," by Ezra Pound.

In "*Tired   I walk toward everything*," the title and italicized lines are from the poem "R E D," by Chase Berggrun.

"Attempting to Speak of Home" is an erasure from the poem "Flight and Metamorphosis," by Nelly Sachs (trans. from the German by Joshua Weiner with Linda B. Parshall).

In "Summer along the Stonycreek," the italicized line is taken from the poem "High Desert, New Mexico," by Kim Addonizio.

"After Ruin" cento contains source poems from Malachi Black ("Sifting in the Afternoon"), Robert Bly ("Living at the End of Time"), Rachael Boast ("Disfigurations"), Mahmoud Darwish ("To a Young Poet"), Dan Gerber ("Often I Imagine the Earth"), Robin Gow ("Sacrament 1"), Chloe Honum ("Spring"), Luther Hughes ("Stay Safe"); Susan Kelly-Dewitt ("Reading Saint John of the Cross"), John Koethe ("Murray Gell-Mann"), Joy Ladin ("Forgetting"), Sylvia Legris ("Gazetteer of the Backyard"), John McAuliffe ("The Ax"), Spencer Reece ("At Thomas Merton's Grave" and "ICU"), James Schuyler ("Scarlatti" and "Sweet Romanian Tongue"), and Eleanor Wilner ("Encounter in the Local Pub").

"Against Consolation" is an erasure from "Working in the Garden, I Think of My Son," by Danusha Laméris.

ABOUT THE AUTHOR

Barbara Sabol was raised in Pennsylvania coal and steel country, a place that has strongly influenced both her values and her writing. She attended the University of Massachusetts and enjoyed a long career as a speech pathologist. Barbara has been writing poetry for more than 25 years, and holds an MFA from Spalding University.

Her fifth book, *Connections: core & all: haiku* (Bird Dog Press, 2022) is part of a dual collection of short-form Japanese poems. Barbara won the Sheila-Na-Gig Editions Poetry Prize in 2019 for her book, *Imagine a Town*. She went on to become the associate editor of *Sheila-Na-Gig online* and edited the anthology *Sharing This Delicate Bread: Selections from Sheila-Na-Gig online* (Sheila-Na-Gig Editions, 2022). Her awards include an Individual Excellence Award from the Ohio Arts Council and the Mary Jean Irion Poetry Prize. She conducts poetry workshops through Literary Cleveland. When not at her desk, Barbara is walking the trails of the Cuyahoga Valley National Park or traveling the country in a restored camper van. She lives in Akron, Ohio, with her husband and wonder dogs.

ACKNOWLEDGMENTS

We are grateful to the editors of the following journals and anthologies in which these poems first appeared:

The Copperfield Review: "Clara Barton Reports from the Field"

Escape into Life: "A Pool of Tears," "Miss Elizabeth Bryan," "Clara Barton at Her Dressing Table," "The Errant Husband," and "I Washed into the World"

Footnote: A Literary Journal of History: "John Hess Ties the Engine Whistle Down" and "Colonel Unger, Returning to the Clubhouse"

I Thought I Heard a Cardinal Sing: Ohio's Appalachian Voices: "The Stargazer" and "Summer along the Stonycreek"

Impost: A Journal of Creative and Critical Work: "Fishing the Stonycreek" and "Keeping an Eye on the River"

Mezzo Cammin: "Once the Floodwaters Recede" and "Ballad of the Makeshift Morgue"

Northern Appalachia Review: "The Drifter," "The Scullery Maid," "The Carpenter," and "John Hess' Last Day"

The Orchards Poetry Journal: "As the Storm Bears Down," "By Noon, That Last Day of May 1889," and "The Saints Have Faces of Stone"

Pandemic Evolution: Poets Respond to the Art of Matthew Wolfe: "Out of Ruin"

Sheila-Na-Gig online: "Tired   I walk toward everything"

Still: The Journal: "At the Plot of the Unknowns"

Unbroken Journal (Right Hand Pointing): "After Ruin"

Women Speak: Women of Appalachia Anthology: "Waterwheel" and "Next to me"

AUTHOR THANKS

The heart and soul of this book came from those things left behind after the flood of 1889—artifacts such as the original morgue book, a large clothbound ledger written in meticulous script, which listed, by morgue and body number, both identified and unidentified victims of The Great Flood. Reading descriptions of the unidentified victims moved me to shape the book around those "unknowns," offering a semblance of a life and voice, albeit invented. I am indebted to Colleen Curry at the Johnstown Flood National Memorial for allowing me access to the book, and to Doug Bosley of the National Park Service, who shared his broad knowledge of the history of the flood, particularly telegraphy along the railway lines. I also wish to thank Andrew Lang, curator of the Johnstown Flood Museum, for granting me access to personal artifacts, such as a porcelain doll, glasses, gloves, letters. Handling each item was deeply moving. Heartfelt gratitude to my poetry partner and dear friend, Marion Starling Boyer, for her keen eye and affection for the characters in the book. She offered valuable feedback on nearly every iteration of these poems. To Professor Marcela Sulak, whose consultation and review of the manuscript led me to reenvision how the figures would best be portrayed. I am honored by Marcela's blurb, as well as those of Sean Thomas Dougherty, William Scott Hanna, Larry Smith, and Jerry Wemple. I admire their work and am thankful for their friendship. To Bob Kline, good friend and train aficionado, whose knowledge of the history of the rail system guided me through narration about the trains, integral to the flood story. If one can be grateful to a place, I thank my hometown, Johnstown, and its people, for the buoyant spirit that brought the city through three major floods. And, never least, to my husband, Tom, whose support and encouragement helped me put my passion project onto these pages.

COLOPHON

The edition you are holding is the First Edition of this publication.

The serif ligature title font is set in Glitten All Caps, created by BrandSemut. The secondary title font and page numbers are set in Avería, created by Dan Sayers. The Alternating Current Press logo is set in Portmanteau, created by JLH Fonts. The foreword signature is set in Azzury Script, created by Akifatype. The wave text symbol is set in Microsoft Himalaya. The roman cover text is set in Athelas, created by Veronika Burian and José Scaglione. All other text is set in Calisto MT, created by Ron Carpenter. All fonts used with permission and full commercial license; all rights reserved.

Cover jacket designed by Leah Angstman, with artwork by Stefan Schweihofer and 1889 map by Alex Y. Lee. The Alternating Current lightbulb logo was created by Leah Angstman, ©2013, 2023 Alternating Current. The front and back endpiece image by Marek Matecki, rain image by Benjamin Nelan, wave image by PublicDomainPictures, carry image by Pexels, flow image by Michaela Kranich, and cover watercolor are all governed under a Pixabay Content License. "Bird's-eye View of the Conemaugh Valley, from Nineveh to the Lake, Johnstown, Pa.: From Personal Sketches and Surveys of the Pennsylvania R. R., by Permission," drawn by Alex Y. Lee for the Pennsylvania Railroad, 1889, courtesy of the Library of Congress Geography and Map Division, loc.gov/item/2010588930. Author photo by Melanie Rae Buonavolonta. All images used with permission and full commercial license; all rights reserved.

Other Works from
ALTERNATING CURRENT PRESS

All of these books (and more) are available at
Alternating Current's website: altcurrentpress.com.

altcurrentpress.com

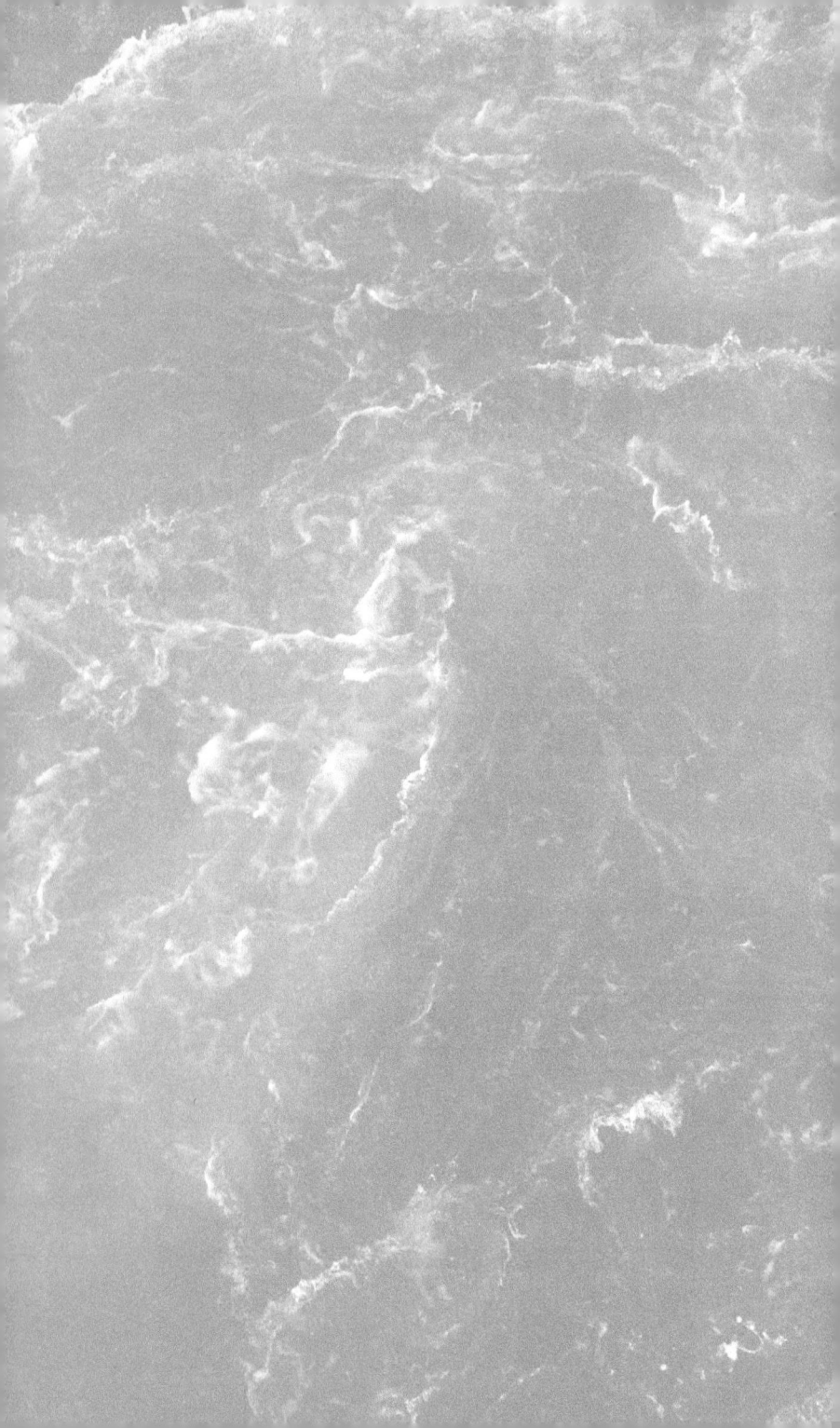